DU
LIBRARY SERVICE
KU-337-327

MUSICAL INSTRUMENTS OF THE WORLD

Percussion

M. J. Knight

W
FRANKLIN WATTS

Schools Library and Information Services

S00000714319

 An Appleseed Editions book

Paperback edition 2006

Franklin Watts
338 Euston Road
London NW1 3BH

Franklin Watts Australia
Hachette Children's Books
Level 17/207 Kent Street
Sydney NSW 2000

© Appleseed Editions, first published 2005

ISBN-10: 0 7496 6984 5
ISBN-13: 978 0 7496 6984 3

Dewey Classification: 786.8

Designed by Helen James
Created by Appleseed Editions Ltd, Well House,
Friars Hill, Guestling, East Sussex TN35 4ET

DUDLEY PUBLIC LIBRARIES

L

714319 | SCH

J 789

All rights reserved. No part of this publication may be reproduced, stored in a retrieval system or transmitted in any form or by any means, electronic, mechanical, photocopy, recording or otherwise, without the prior written permission of the copyright owner.

A CIP catalogue for this book is available from the British Library.

Photographs by Corbis (Paul Almasy, Australian Picture Library, Michelle Chaplow, GILBERT LIZ/CORBIS SYGMA, Pablo Corral V, Philip James Corwin, Derick A. Thomas; Dat's Jazz, Michael Freeman, Anthony Bannister; Gallo Images, Lindsay Hebberd, Dave G. Houser, Wolfgang Kaehler, James Marshall, Gideon Mendel, Tim Mosenfelder, Carl & Ann Purcell, Royalty-Free, Pete Saloutos, Norbert Schaefer, Michael St. Maur Sheil, Vince Streano, Tim Wright), The Lebrecht Collection

Printed in Thailand

Contents

Introducing percussion instruments

percussion

percussion

Τhis book is about the musical instruments that belong to the percussion family.

Percussion instruments sound when you hit, shake or scrape them. Their sounds can be made in many ways. For example, cymbals can be clashed together loudly, or slid gently against each other to make a softer sound. Many percussion instruments create gentle sounds, as well as loud noises.

These Chukka drummers from Kenya beat out a loud and exciting rhythm.

Drums may be the world's oldest musical instruments. People have played them to accompany dancing, battles and ceremonies for thousands of years. Long ago, people thought they could conjure up thunder, or frighten away enemies. Some believed that bells, rattles and shakers had magic powers too.

A group of Indian boys make music with drums, cymbals, clapping and horns.

Every country makes percussion instruments. All modern orchestras have a percussion section, and you can also hear percussion instruments beating out a rhythm in all sorts of other musical ensembles, including folk, dance, jazz, pop and rock bands.

Bass drum

Bass drum
Bass drum
Bass drum
Bass drum

The bass drum in an orchestra is so big the percussionist has to stand up to play it. At just the right moment in the music, he strikes the drum on one side with a beater. He can damp (or quieten) the drum by putting his hand on the other side.

You can hear smaller bass drums played in military bands. The drummer carries his drum against his chest, banging it on both sides with hard felt beaters as he marks time for the marching soldiers. He signals when to stop by playing two fast beats called a double tap.

Did you know?

One of the largest bass drums ever played was built in England in 1857. It measured 240 centimetres across. The largest bass drum ever made is in Disneyland in California. This drum is 320 centimetres across, but it has never been played.

These loud bass drums help the band to march in time with the music.

Kettledrum

Kettledrum

Kettledrum

Kettledrum

Kettledrum

Kettledrum

Timpani can make an orchestra sound very exciting.

These large drums are also called timpani. Orchestras have three or four, each playing a different note.

The bottom half of a kettledrum is made of copper, and is called the bowl, after its shape. The top is the skin, or the head, and is plastic. Each drum has a pedal which you can press to make it sound a higher or lower note.

A timpanist (someone who plays timpani) plays with drumsticks. Some have wooden ends to make a loud sound, and others felt ends for making soft sounds.

Did you know?

Soldiers on horseback, called cavalrymen, first played kettledrums hundreds of years ago. The drums were slung on either side of the horse and the drummer played as he rode along.

Tubular bells
Tubular bells

Tubular bells are not bell-shaped, but they ring like bells when they are played. If you ran a wooden hammer from the longest to the shortest, you would play the notes from the lowest to the highest.

There are 18 tubes in a set of tubular bells, arranged in size order. The longest and lowest are on the left, and the shortest and highest on the right. You sound them by hitting them near the top with small wooden hammers called mallets. You can press a pedal at the bottom called a damper to stop the sound.

Tubular bells hang in a metal frame and vibrate when they are tapped with a mallet.

Claves Claves Claves

Have you ever held a piece of wood in each hand, and tapped them together to make a sound? This is how you play the claves.

Claves are also called percussion sticks. They are sometimes played in an orchestra, but more often they are heard in South American dance music, where they tap out the beat.

Claves are made from two hard, smooth lengths of wood. The player holds one clave cupped in the palm of one hand, and taps it with other to make a bright, sharp crack. It is not as easy as it sounds to keep time!

Paul Simon plays the claves at a concert in Ellis Park Stadium in South Africa.

Cymbals

Cymbals Cymbals

Imagine a pair of cymbals so small you can play them with your thumb and one finger. These are the smallest cymbals in the world, and they are worn by dancers in Asia, Egypt and Greece.

The largest cymbals, by contrast, can measure 65 centimetres across the middle. These cymbals are played in a western orchestra and they have leather hand grips to help the percussionist hold them firmly while playing.

This musician hits two fixed cymbals with the two he holds in his hands. He is part of a gamelan orchestra.

Clashed together, large cymbals can be deafening, but slid across each other, the sound they make is gentler and longer-lasting. For a crisp, sharp sound, tap a cymbal with a drumstick. To stop the sound, hold the edge of the cymbal to stop it vibrating.

This cymbal player clashes his cymbals together to the beat of the drums in a marching band.

Different sorts of cymbals, called chengcheng and rinchik, are played in a gamelan orchestra. These are pairs of cymbals on stands, which the player sounds by hitting them with a second set of cymbals.

Cymbals Cymbals Cymbals

Timbales

Timbales Timbales Timbales Timbales

Dance-band drummers play these shallow metal drums in pairs, using thin wooden drumsticks to create a bright, ringing sound.

Both drums in a pair are the same depth, but they have different diameters (the measurement across the circular top of the drum). This is why they sound different notes. The larger the diameter, the lower the sound made by the drum.

The timbales come from Latin America and you most often hear them beating out a foot-tapping rhythm to dance music.

Jose Chepito plays the timbales alongside other drums at a jazz festival in Holland.

Tabla
Tabla

Tabla
Tabla

The tabla is a pair of drums heard in Indian classical music. They usually accompany two stringed instruments, called a sitar and a tambura.

Tabla drummers sit cross-legged on the floor and play the drums with their fingertips and wrists.

The two drums are different shapes and sizes. The larger one is bowl-shaped and plays low notes, and the smaller is cylindrical and plays higher notes. Tabla can be made of clay or wood.

Musicians in Jaipur in India sit on the floor to play the sitar and tabla drums.

Did you know?

Before starting to play, a tabla player smears the top of each drum with a black paste, which helps to make the sound clear and crisp.

13

Drum kit

Drum kit Drum kit
Drum kit Drum kit

Have you ever wanted to play the drums? Most rock, pop, jazz and dance bands have a drum kit, which plays the beat of the music.

Travis Barker plays the drums for Los Angeles band The Transplants.

14

Biggest and lowest-sounding is the bass drum. The drummer plays it with a foot pedal, which makes a padded beater hit the drum. Next largest is the tenor drum, standing on two legs and played with drumsticks.

A pair of smaller drums called tom-toms sit on a stand above the others. Also on a stand, the snare drum has wires across the bottom which vibrate (or rattle) against the underside of the drum when the drummer hits it.

Drum kits have several cymbals. The ride cymbal is the largest, followed by the hi-hat – two cymbals clashed together with a foot pedal. The third is the crash cymbal.

Drummers play the cymbals with a drumstick or a beater, or, if they want to make a softer sound, with wire brushes.

Drumsticks make the loudest sounds. Brushes and beaters are softer and quieter.

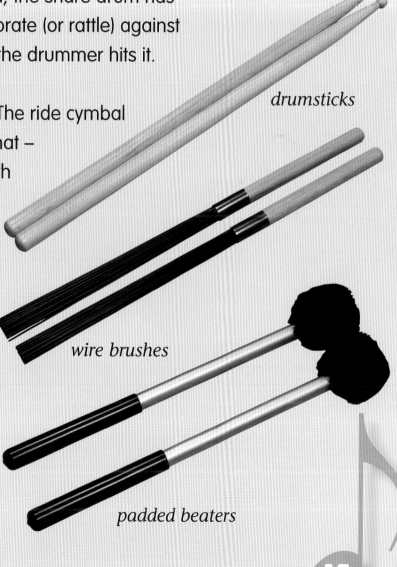

drumsticks

wire brushes

padded beaters

15

Thumb piano

Thumb piano Thumb piano

This African instrument is a series of thin metal strips held in place on a wooden board by a metal rod. Each strip plays a different note and the player sounds them by twanging them with her thumbs.

The thumb piano has other names: the mbira or the sansa. The player can change the note each strip makes by moving it backwards or forwards under the rod. The longer the strip, the lower the note it makes.

The thumb piano is played in many African countries.

Two women play sansa together. They are San people, who live in Botswana and Namibia in Africa.

16

Talking drum

Talking drum

The talking drum looks different from other drums because of the strings which run along its sides. They are tied to the top and bottom of the drum.

To play, you hold the drum under one arm and squeeze the sides in and out, while hitting the top with a curved wooden drumstick.

Squeezing the drum pulls the strings and stretches the skin at the top. As the top stretches, the sound of the drum becomes higher. This is how the drum 'talks'.

This wooden drum is traditionally played in West Africa.

Did you know?

The African name for talking drum is kalungu.

This Nigerian musician squeezes her drum more tightly under her arm when she wants to make a higher note.

Xylophone Xylophone

Xylophone Xylophone

Have you ever played a xylophone? It is a set of tuned wooden bars which look a bit like piano keys. A xylophone player hits the bars with round-ended wooden sticks, to make a ringing sound.

To make the sound louder, large xylophones have metal tubes under the bars, which resonate (or vibrate) when the bar is hit. Smaller xylophones have a hollow wooden box underneath.

These children are learning to play the xylophone in Tokyo, Japan.

There are many different kinds of xylophone. Log xylophones are traditional African instruments. Some have hollowed-out gourds (fruit like small pumpkins) underneath the bars.

The marimba is a large xylophone played in Central America and Africa. It has mellow, light tone, and is so big that three people can play it at once.

Three men at a time can play these large marimbas in Guatemala, Central America.

Did you know?

A xylophone from Sierra Leone in West Africa has holes in the hollow gourds under the bars. These are covered with silk from the egg cases of spiders, which gives the xylophone a buzzing sound.

19

Bongos

Bongos Bongos

Bongo players hold their drums between their knees and beat out a high-pitched rhythm using their fingers and thumbs.

Bongos are always played in pairs, with the larger, deeper-sounding drum on the player's right-hand side. The two drums are joined by a brace. To make a louder sound, the drummer can hit them with wooden drumsticks.

Bongos came originally from Latin America. Listen for their high-pitched beat in Latin American dance music and pop music.

The larger of the two bongo drums is always on the player's right.

Did you know?

In Cuba, bongos are made from short sections of hollow tree trunk, with skins nailed over the wider end.

20

Bodhran Bodhran Bodhran

You can hear bodhrans marking the rhythm of the traditional songs and dances played in Irish folk music. This type of drum is called a frame drum because it is made from a hoop-shaped wooden frame with a skin stretched across the top.

To play the bodhran you hold it in your left hand, and beat the skin with the fingers of your right hand, or with a double-headed drumstick.

Frame drums are played all over the world, from Europe to the Middle East.

Did you know?

A tambourine is a frame drum with jingles set in the sides.

This Irish boy is playing the bodhran at a music festival in Ireland.

Steel drums
Steel drums

Sixty years ago, islanders in the Caribbean discovered they could make musical instruments from oil drums. This is how steel drums began.

The St Christopher steel band play in the Caribbean.

The bright, tinny sound of a steel drum band comes from several different drums. Largest are the bass drums, each made from a whole oil drum with the bottom cut off. These play the lowest notes.

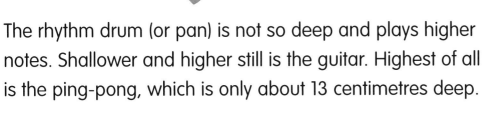

Steel drums

The rhythm drum (or pan) is not so deep and plays higher notes. Shallower and higher still is the guitar. Highest of all is the ping-pong, which is only about 13 centimetres deep.

1 *A drum maker bashes the end of an oil barrel into a curved shape with a sledgehammer.*

2 *A pattern is traced on the top of the drum. A bass drum has five sections, a rhythm drum two, a guitar nine, and a ping-pong 25.*

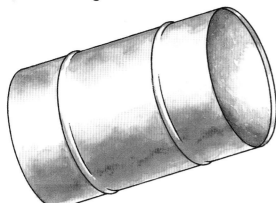

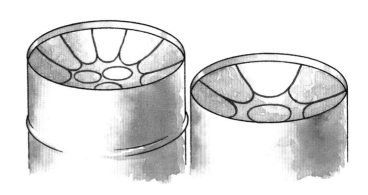

3 *The drum maker follows the pattern to raise thousands of tiny marks on the drum with a nail punch. Then the drum is cut to the right depth.*

4 *The drum is heated over a fire, then plunged into cold water to make it stronger. Finally it is tuned and decorated.*

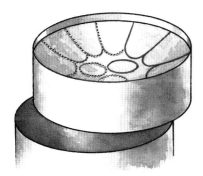

Glockenspiel

Glockenspiel Glockenspiel Glockenspiel

Have you heard a glockenspiel? The metal bars of this instrument make a clear, bell-like sound when you hit them. The bars are arranged in a similar way to the keys on a piano.

When a glockenspiel is played in an orchestra, the percussionist hits the bars with two beaters which have hard, rounded ends. You can also hear glockenspiels played in marching bands. When it is carried in a band, a glockenspiel is held upright so that the bars face the player.

Did you know?

Glockenspiel is a German word which means bell play.

The girls in this Thai band are playing upright glockenspiels.

Triangle ♪

Which shape is also a musical instrument? The triangle. This simple instrument is a bent steel rod with a small gap between the two ends. The gap lets the triangle vibrate or ring when the player hits it with a metal beater.

Tapped gently, the triangle makes a quiet sound. To make it louder, the player moves the beater quickly from side to side. Its sound is high and tinkling.

Triangles usually hang from a thread or strap so they can vibrate freely. Orchestras have triangles of various sizes which each play a different note.

You can start playing the triangle when you are very young.

Bonang Bonang Bonang

Bonang players performing in a gamelan orchestra in Java, Indonesia.

A bonang looks like deep-sided cooking pots sitting on a carved wooden frame.

Each gong has a raised area in the middle called the boss. This is the part the bonang player hits with soft-ended beaters, making a soft, bell-like sound.

This Javanese instrument is part of a gamelan orchestra. The bonang accompanies other instruments, which play the tune in a piece of traditional music. It is also called a gong chime.

Gamelan orchestra

Gamelan orchestra

Indonesian orchestras are called gamelans. Most of the instruments in this sort of orchestra are percussion instruments.

In a gamelan orchestra there are gongs, xylophones, metallophones, cymbals and gong chimes. Other instruments in the orchestra are a bamboo flute called a suling, a two-string fiddle called a rebab, and box-shaped stringed instruments called zithers.

Did you know?

The musicians in a gamelan orchestra always play from memory. Musicians in a western orchestra always have written music in front of them during a performance.

There are usually about 30 instruments in the orchestra. Together they create a rich and intricate sound when they play on important occasions and at religious ceremonies. Gamelan orchestras also play music for plays or puppet shows.

A gamelan orchestra plays at the ceremonial dance of the dragon in Bali, Indonesia.

27

Castanets

Castanets Castanets Castanets

Have you seen flamenco dancing? In this dramatic Spanish dance the performers hold pairs of castanets in their hands, and click to the rhythm as they dance.

Castanets are always played in pairs. Dancers click a higher-sounding pair of castanets with their right hand and a larger, lower-sounding pair in their left while they dance.

This flamenco dancer holds a pair of castanets high over her head.

28

Castanets are a type of clapper. They have been played in different parts of the world for thousands of years. Today castanets are usually made from a single piece of wood and shaped like a pair of shells. The two halves are held together by a cord.

Orchestral castanets are attached to a handle, which the player shakes with one hand, while hitting the shells against their other hand.

Dancers hook the castanets over a thumb and click them together with their fingers.

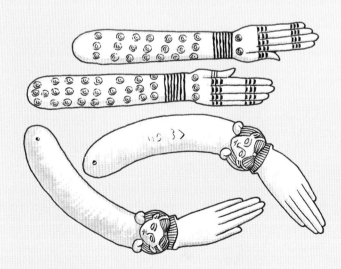

Clappers in the shape of hands were made in Ancient Egypt thousands of years ago.

Did you know?

Some of the first clappers were made from hippopotamus teeth and played in Egypt around 4,000 years ago.

Words to remember

accompany To play music alongside a singer or another musician who is playing the tune.

beat The steady pulse, or rhythm, of music.

beaters Wooden or wire sticks used to tap or hit some instruments.

bowl The round, deep body of a drum.

classical music Serious music is sometimes called classical music to separate it from popular music. Classical music can also mean music which was written during the late 18th and early 19th centuries and followed certain rules.

cylindrical Shaped like a cylinder – the same shape as a tin can.

folk music Traditional songs and tunes which are so old that no one remembers who wrote them.

gamelan orchestra A group of instruments from Indonesia played in religious ceremonies. It can include percussion instruments, drums, fiddles and flutes.

head The part of a drum which is hit or struck. It is also called the skin.

jazz A type of music played by a group of instruments in which each one plays its own tune. Jazz musicians often improvise, or make up, the tunes they play.

marching band A group of musicians who march along as they play. Most marching bands play music which was originally played by soldiers.

mellow Gentle and warm.

metallophone An instrument which looks like a xylophone but has metal bars rather than wooden ones. Metallophones play an important part in a gamelan orchestra.

musician Someone who plays an instrument or sings.

oil drum A large cylindrical metal container for storing oil.

orchestra A large group of musicians playing together.

pedal Part of an instrument worked by foot.

percussionist Someone who plays a percussion instrument.

pitch How low or high a sound is.

pop music Popular music which is entertaining and easy to listen to.

rhythm The beat of the music, which depends on how short or long the notes are.

rock music Pop music with a strong beat, or rhythm.

skin The part of a drum which is hit or struck. It is also called the head.

vibrate To move up and down very quickly, or quiver.

Index